DON'T
WORRY
BE
HAPPY

summersdale

DON'T WORRY BE HAPPY

Summersdale Publishers Ltd
46 West Street
Chichester
West Sussex
PO19 1RP
UK

www.summersdale.com

Printed and bound in the Czech Republic

ISBN: 978-1-84953-688-2

Substantial discounts on bulk quantities of Summersdale books are available to corporations, professional associations and other organisations. For details contact Nicky Douglas by telephone: +44 (0) 1243 756902, fax: +44 (0) 1243 786300 or email: nicky@summersdale.com.

TO..

FROM..

SHOOT FOR THE
MOON. EVEN IF YOU
MISS, YOU'LL LAND
AMONG THE STARS.

Les Brown

HAPPINESS NEVER DECREASES BY BEING SHARED.

Buddha

SOMETIMES
YOU'VE GOT
TO LET GO OF
THE GOOD TO
MAKE WAY FOR
THE GREAT!

LIFE IS VERY INTERESTING IF YOU MAKE MISTAKES.

Georges Carpentier

LAUGHING MAKES EVERYTHING EASIER.

Carmen Electra

MAKE A DECISION
TO MAKE
YOUR DREAMS
COME TRUE

THINK OF ALL THE BEAUTY STILL LEFT AROUND YOU AND BE HAPPY.

Anne Frank

PLEASURE IN THE
JOB PUTS PERFECTION
IN THE WORK.

Aristotle

FOCUS ON
SOMEONE, OR
SOMETHING, TO
LOVE EACH DAY

IT'S ALL RIGHT TO
HAVE BUTTERFLIES
IN YOUR STOMACH.
JUST GET THEM TO
FLY IN FORMATION.

Rob Gilbert

LIVE ALL YOU CAN;
IT'S A MISTAKE
NOT TO.

Henry James

LIFE IS TOO SHORT TO SWEAT THE SMALL STUFF

WHEN ASKED IF MY
CUP IS HALF-FULL OR
HALF-EMPTY MY ONLY
RESPONSE IS THAT I AM
THANKFUL I HAVE A CUP.

Sam Lefkowitz

TO SUCCEED IN LIFE, YOU
NEED THREE THINGS: A
WISHBONE, A BACKBONE
AND A FUNNYBONE.

Reba McEntire

RAIN OR
SHINE, IT'S A
BEAUTIFUL DAY

THE MOST EFFECTIVE WAY TO DO IT IS TO DO IT.

Amelia Earhart

LAUGHTER GIVES US
DISTANCE. IT ALLOWS
US TO STEP BACK FROM
AN EVENT, DEAL WITH
IT AND THEN MOVE ON.

Bob Newhart

EVERYTHING YOU
NEED IS ALREADY
INSIDE YOU

ALL LIFE IS AN EXPERIMENT.

Ralph Waldo Emerson

WHATEVER IS GOING
TO HAPPEN WILL
HAPPEN, WHETHER
WE WORRY OR NOT.

Ana Monnar

IF YOU CAN
THINK ABOUT
WORRIES,
YOU CAN
THINK ABOUT
HAPPINESS

ALWAYS LAUGH
WHEN YOU CAN. IT IS
CHEAP MEDICINE.

Lord Byron

NOTHING REALLY
MATTERS EXCEPT WHAT
YOU DO NOW IN THIS
INSTANT OF TIME.

Eileen Caddy

NEVER GIVE UP.
GREAT THINGS
TAKE TIME

IT AIN'T NO USE PUTTING
UP YOUR UMBRELLA
TILL IT RAINS.

Alice Hegan Rice

DO WHAT YOU CAN,
WITH WHAT YOU HAVE,
WHERE YOU ARE.

Theodore Roosevelt

EVERYTHING HAPPENS FOR A REASON

ISN'T IT NICE TO THINK
THAT TOMORROW IS
A NEW DAY WITH NO
MISTAKES IN IT YET?

L. M. Montgomery

HE WHO NEVER MAKES MISTAKES, NEVER MAKES ANYTHING.

English proverb

DON'T LISTEN
TO THE VOICES
IN YOUR HEAD.
LISTEN TO
YOUR HEART

SOME DAYS THERE WON'T
BE A SONG IN YOUR
HEART. SING ANYWAY.

Emory Austin

I'D RATHER REGRET THE
THINGS I'VE DONE THAN
REGRET THE THINGS
I HAVEN'T DONE.

Lucille Ball

CHANGE IS AN OPPORTUNITY IN DISGUISE

SOME PEOPLE ARE
ALWAYS GRUMBLING
BECAUSE ROSES
HAVE THORNS; I AM
THANKFUL THAT
THORNS HAVE ROSES.

Jean-Baptiste Alphonse Karr

DON'T WORRY ABOUT IT. THE RIGHT THING WILL COME AT THE RIGHT TIME.

Danielle Steel

WHEN YOU NEED SOMETHING TO BELIEVE IN, START WITH YOURSELF

WORRY IS A MISUSE OF THE IMAGINATION.

Dan Zadra

I AM AN OLD MAN AND
HAVE KNOWN A GREAT
MANY TROUBLES,
BUT MOST OF THEM
NEVER HAPPENED.

Mark Twain

GIVE UP BEING PERFECT AND JUST BE YOURSELF

IF YOU CAN'T LAUGH,
YOU WON'T MAKE IT.

Jennifer Love Hewitt

WHEN LIFE LOOKS
LIKE IT'S FALLING
APART, IT MAY JUST BE
FALLING IN PLACE.

Beverly Solomon

YOU ARE
ALLOWED
TO CHANGE
YOUR MIND

TO ERR IS HUMAN, TO FORGIVE, DIVINE.

Alexander Pope

DON'T WORRY ABOUT
THE WORLD COMING
TO AN END TODAY. IT IS
ALREADY TOMORROW
IN AUSTRALIA.

Charles M. Schulz

WHAT ARE
YOU GOING TO
DO WITH THIS
BRAND NEW DAY?

THE WAY I SEE IT, IF YOU WANT THE RAINBOW, YOU GOTTA PUT UP WITH THE RAIN.

Dolly Parton

NOT A SHRED OF
EVIDENCE EXISTS IN
FAVOUR OF THE IDEA
THAT LIFE IS SERIOUS.

Brendan Gill

NOTHING CAN
HOLD YOU BACK

LIFE IS A ROLLER COASTER. TRY TO EAT A LIGHT LUNCH.

David A. Schmaltz

HAPPINESS IS NOT A GOAL; IT IS A BY-PRODUCT.

Eleanor Roosevelt

THERE'S NO
TIME LIKE THE
PRESENT

LIFE ISN'T ABOUT
WAITING FOR THE
STORM TO PASS... IT'S
ABOUT LEARNING TO
DANCE IN THE RAIN.

Vivian Greene

WORRY IS A DIVIDEND PAID TO DISASTER BEFORE IT IS DUE.

Ian Fleming

SOMETIMES THE
WRONG CHOICES
BRING US TO THE
RIGHT PLACES

IT IS NOT HOW MUCH
WE HAVE, BUT HOW
MUCH WE ENJOY, THAT
MAKES HAPPINESS.

Charles Spurgeon

IT IS OF IMMENSE
IMPORTANCE TO
LEARN TO LAUGH
AT OURSELVES.

Katherine Mansfield

BE TRUE, BE
YOU, PUT LOVE
IN WHAT YOU DO

RELEASE YOUR
STRUGGLE, LET GO OF
YOUR MIND, THROW AWAY
YOUR CONCERNS, AND
RELAX INTO THE WORLD.

Dan Millman

HAPPINESS CONSISTS
NOT IN HAVING MUCH,
BUT IN BEING CONTENT
WITH LITTLE.

Marguerite Gardiner

REMEMBER,
90 PER CENT
OF WHAT YOU
WORRY ABOUT
NEVER HAPPENS

LET US BE OF GOOD
CHEER, REMEMBERING
THAT THE MISFORTUNES
HARDEST TO BEAR
ARE THOSE WHICH
NEVER HAPPEN.

James Russell Lowell

WORRYING IS USING
YOUR IMAGINATION TO
CREATE SOMETHING
YOU DON'T WANT.

Esther Hicks

ASK YOURSELF,
WILL THIS
MATTER A YEAR
FROM NOW?

WORRY NEVER ROBS
TOMORROW OF ITS
SORROW, IT ONLY SAPS
TODAY OF ITS JOY.

Leo Buscaglia

BE HAPPY. IT'S ONE WAY OF BEING WISE.

Colette

IMAGINE.
BELIEVE.
ACHIEVE.

SOME DAYS YOU'RE
A BUG. SOME DAYS
YOU'RE A WINDSHIELD.

Price Cobb

REAL LIFE SEEMS TO HAVE NO PLOTS.

Ivy Compton-Burnett

JUST TAKE THE
FIRST STEP

SAY AND DO SOMETHING
POSITIVE THAT WILL
HELP THE SITUATION;
IT DOESN'T TAKE ANY
BRAINS TO COMPLAIN.

Robert A. Cook

WHEN YOU COME TO A ROADBLOCK, TAKE A DETOUR.

Mary Kay Ash

TAKE LIFE ONE
DAY AT A TIME

IF YOU CAN FIND A PATH
WITH NO OBSTACLES,
IT PROBABLY DOESN'T
LEAD ANYWHERE.

Frank A. Clark

WORK ON WHAT IS REAL
RATHER THAN WORRY
ABOUT WHAT IS UNREAL.

Elizabeth George

DO SMALL THINGS WITH GREAT LOVE

WE NEED TO BE THE
CHANGE WE WISH TO
SEE IN THE WORLD.

Mahatma Gandhi

NEVER LOOK BACKWARDS
OR YOU'LL FALL
DOWN THE STAIRS.

Rudyard Kipling

TODAY IS THE
TOMORROW YOU
WORRIED ABOUT
YESTERDAY

FOR MYSELF I AM AN
OPTIMIST – IT DOES NOT
SEEM TO BE MUCH USE
BEING ANYTHING ELSE.

Winston Churchill

WORRY IS AS USELESS AS A HANDLE ON A SNOWBALL.

Mitzi Chandler

LAUGHTER
IS THE BEST
MEDICINE AND
IT HAS NO SIDE
EFFECTS

IN THE MIDDLE OF DIFFICULTY LIES OPPORTUNITY.

Albert Einstein

YOU'RE WORRIED
ABOUT WHAT-IFS.
WELL, WHAT IF YOU
STOPPED WORRYING?

Shannon Celebi

STRIVE FOR
PROGRESS, NOT
PERFECTION

AT THE HEIGHT OF
LAUGHTER, THE
UNIVERSE IS FLUNG
INTO A KALEIDOSCOPE
OF NEW POSSIBILITIES.

Jean Houston

YOUR ATTITUDE IS LIKE
A BOX OF CRAYONS THAT
COLOUR YOUR WORLD.

Allen Klein

THERE IS
ALWAYS A WAY

THE PURPOSE OF LIFE IS TO BE HAPPY.

Dalai Lama

THE MAN WHO REMOVES
A MOUNTAIN BEGINS
BY CARRYING AWAY
SMALL STONES.

Chinese proverb

LET GO OF THE
PAST, ENJOY
THE PRESENT
AND EMBRACE
THE FUTURE

ERRORS ARE VOLITIONAL
AND ARE THE PORTALS
OF DISCOVERY.

James Joyce

KEEPING BUSY AND
MAKING OPTIMISM
A WAY OF LIFE CAN
RESTORE YOUR FAITH
IN YOURSELF.

Lucille Ball

DO NOT WAIT FOR
PERFECT. ENJOY
YOUR LIFE

IF THINGS GO WRONG, DON'T GO WITH THEM.

Roger Babson

HAPPINESS ARISES IN A STATE OF PEACE, NOT OF TUMULT.

Ann Radcliffe

MAKE YOUR
DAYS COUNT

WORRY IS BLIND, AND CANNOT DISCERN THE FUTURE.

Ellen G. White

WHAT MATTERS IS TO
LIVE IN THE PRESENT,
LIVE NOW, FOR EVERY
MOMENT IS NOW.

Sathya Sai Baba

SOMETIMES
OUR BIGGEST
FAILURES LEAD
TO OUR BIGGEST
SUCCESSES

LIFE IS A SHIPWRECK,
BUT WE MUST NOT
FORGET TO SING IN
THE LIFEBOATS.

Voltaire

A GOOD LAUGH IS
SUNSHINE IN
THE HOUSE.

William Makepeace Thackeray

DO SOMETHING TODAY JUST FOR THE FUN OF IT

AGAINST THE ASSAULT OF LAUGHTER NOTHING CAN STAND.

Mark Twain

WITH THE NEW DAY
COMES NEW STRENGTH
AND NEW THOUGHTS.

Eleanor Roosevelt

WORRYING
NEVER CHANGES
THE OUTCOME

IF YOU CAN SOLVE
YOUR PROBLEM, THEN
WHAT IS THE NEED
OF WORRYING? IF
YOU CANNOT SOLVE IT,
THEN WHAT IS THE
USE OF WORRYING?

Śāntideva

TO ME, EVERY HOUR
OF THE DAY AND NIGHT
IS AN UNSPEAKABLY
PERFECT MIRACLE.

Walt Whitman

GIVE YOURSELF
PERMISSION TO
START AGAIN

DON'T GET YOUR
KNICKERS IN A KNOT.
NOTHING IS SOLVED
AND IT JUST MAKES
YOU WALK FUNNY.

Kathryn Carpenter

MOST FOLKS ARE ABOUT
AS HAPPY AS THEY MAKE
UP THEIR MINDS TO BE.

Abraham Lincoln

EVERY
CHALLENGE IS
AN OPPORTUNITY
TO LEARN

WORRY IS LIKE A
SQUATTER: IT SNEAKS
IN AND TRIES TO STAY
WITHOUT PAYING
RENT! SERVE IT
EVICTION PAPERS!

Evinda Lepins

THERE IS LITTLE
SUCCESS WHERE THERE
IS LITTLE LAUGHTER.

Andrew Carnegie

STAY OPEN TO
POSSIBILITIES

WORRY IS AN OLD
MAN WITH A BENT
HEAD, CARRYING A
LOAD OF FEATHERS
HE THINKS IS LEAD.

Billy Graham

LIFE IS LIKE PHOTOGRAPHY; WE DEVELOP FROM THE NEGATIVES.

Anonymous

IF YOU BELIEVE
IN YOURSELF,
ANYTHING IS
POSSIBLE

WORRY DOES NOT KEEP
IT FROM RAINING
TOMORROW, BUT IT
DOES KEEP IT FROM
BEING SUNNY TODAY.

Shannon L. Alder

ALL THE STATISTICS IN THE WORLD CAN'T MEASURE THE WARMTH OF A SMILE.

Chris Hart

SING YOUR
OWN SONG!

REGARD MISTAKES AS TEACHERS, NOT JUDGES!

Tae Yun Kim

TO TRAVEL HOPEFULLY
IS A BETTER THING
THAN TO ARRIVE, AND
THE TRUE SUCCESS
IS TO LABOUR.

Robert Louis Stevenson

YOU ARE EXACTLY
WHERE YOU ARE
SUPPOSED TO BE

THERE ARE ALWAYS
FLOWERS FOR THOSE
WHO WANT TO SEE THEM.

Henri Matisse

WORRY OFTEN GIVES A SMALL THING A BIG SHADOW.

Swedish proverb

SURROUND
YOURSELF
WITH PEOPLE
WHO MAKE
YOU SMILE

HAPPINESS IS A WAY OF TRAVEL – NOT A DESTINATION.

Roy M. Goodman

GIVE LIGHT, AND
THE DARKNESS WILL
DISAPPEAR OF ITSELF.

Desiderius Erasmus

THE ONLY TIME
YOU SHOULD
EVER LOOK
BACK IS TO SEE
HOW FAR YOU
HAVE COME!

IF YOU'RE GOING TO
WALK ON THIN ICE, YOU
MIGHT AS WELL DANCE.

Anonymous

LAUGHTER IS THE SUN
THAT DRIVES WINTER
FROM THE HUMAN FACE.

Victor Hugo

WORRY IS
NOTHING
MORE THAN A
BAD HABIT

ONCE YOU REPLACE
NEGATIVE THOUGHTS
WITH POSITIVE ONES,
YOU'LL START HAVING
POSITIVE RESULTS.

Willie Nelson

SMOOTH SEAS DO NOT
MAKE SKILFUL SAILORS.

African proverb

LET GO AND
LIGHTEN UP!

NOTHING IS A WASTE OF TIME IF YOU USE THE EXPERIENCE WISELY.

Auguste Rodin

DO NOT ANTICIPATE
TROUBLE, OR WORRY
ABOUT WHAT MAY
NEVER HAPPEN. KEEP
IN THE SUNLIGHT.

Benjamin Franklin

WHEN YOU'RE
BLOWING THINGS
OUT OF PROPORTION,
REMEMBER YOU'RE
THE ONE DOING
THE BLOWING

WHOEVER IS HAPPY
WILL MAKE OTHERS
HAPPY TOO.

Anne Frank

IF YOU HAVE GOOD
THOUGHTS THEY WILL
SHINE OUT OF YOUR
FACE LIKE SUNBEAMS
AND YOU WILL ALWAYS
LOOK LOVELY.

Roald Dahl

IT'S ONLY IN
DARK OF NIGHT
THAT YOU CAN
SEE THE STARS

WORRY IS LIKE A
ROCKING-CHAIR. IT GIVES
YOU SOMETHING TO DO
BUT GETS YOU NOWHERE.

Wayne Bennett

REAL DIFFICULTIES CAN
BE OVERCOME, IT IS
ONLY THE IMAGINARY
ONES THAT ARE
UNCONQUERABLE.

Theodore Newton Vail

FOCUS ON WHAT
YOU WANT, NOT
ON WHAT YOU
DON'T WANT!

LET GO OF YOUR
WORRIES AND FOCUS
ONLY ON THE TASK AT
HAND. THE FUTURE
WILL BE WHAT IT WILL.

Christopher Paolini

MEN'S BEST SUCCESSES
COME AFTER THEIR
DISAPPOINTMENTS.

Henry Ward Beecher

DO ONE THING
EVERY DAY
THAT MAKES
YOU HAPPY

WORRY IS THE DARKROOM IN WHICH NEGATIVES CAN DEVELOP.

Wanda E. Brunstetter

THEREFORE DO
NOT WORRY ABOUT
TOMORROW, FOR
TOMORROW WILL WORRY
ABOUT ITS OWN THINGS.

Matthew 6:34

SLOW DOWN SO
HAPPINESS CAN
CATCH YOU UP

MIX A LITTLE
FOOLISHNESS WITH YOUR
SERIOUS PLANS. IT IS
LOVELY TO BE SILLY AT
THE RIGHT MOMENT.

Horace

LOOK AT LIFE THROUGH
THE WINDSHIELD, NOT
THE REAR-VIEW MIRROR.

Byrd Baggett

LET IT GO,
AND MOVE ON

I MAY NOT HAVE GONE
WHERE I INTENDED...
BUT I THINK I HAVE
ENDED UP WHERE
I NEEDED TO BE.

Douglas Adams

IT IS NEVER TOO LATE
TO BE WHAT YOU
MIGHT HAVE BEEN.

George Eliot

NEVER FORGET
TO BE YOURSELF

Meet Esme!

Our feathered friend Esme loves finding perfect quotes for the perfect occasion, and is almost as good at collecting them as she is at collecting twigs for her nest. She's always full of joy and happiness, singing her messages of goodwill in this series of uplifting, heart-warming books.

Follow Esme on Twitter at **@EsmeTheBird**.

For more information about our books,
find us on Facebook at **Summersdale Publishers**
and follow us on Twitter at **@Summersdale**.

www.summersdale.com